Managing Your Product Manager Career

How Product Managers Can Find And Succeed In The Right Job

"Practical, proven examples of how to secure the right product management job and be a success!"

Dr. Jim Anderson

Published by:
Blue Elephant Consulting
Tampa, Florida

Copyright © 2016 by Dr. Jim Anderson

All rights reserved. No part of this book may be reproduced of transmitted in any form or by any means, electronic or mechanical, including photocopying, recording or by any information storage and retrieval system without written permission of the publisher, except for inclusion of brief quotations in a review.

Printed in the United States of America

Library of Congress Control Number: 2016920060

ISBN-13: 978-1540757920
ISBN-10: 1540757927

Warning – Disclaimer

The purpose of this book is to educate and entertain. This book does not promise or guarantee that anyone following the ideas, tips, suggestions, techniques or strategies will be successful. The author, publisher and distributor(s) shall have neither liability nor responsibility to anyone with respect to any loss or damage caused, or alleged to be caused, directly or indirectly by the information contained in this book.

Recent Books By The Author

Product Management

- How Product Managers Can Sell More Of Their Product: Tips & Techniques For Product Managers To Better Understand How To Sell Their Product

- Product Development Lessons For Product Managers: How Product Managers Can Create Successful Products

Public Speaking

- Changing How You Speak To Overcome Your Fear Of Speaking: Change techniques that will transform a speech into a memorable event

- Delivering Excellence: How To Give Presentations That Make A Difference: Presentation techniques that will transform a speech into a memorable event

CIO Skills

- Keeping The Barbarians Out: How CIOs Can Secure Their Department and Company: Tips And Techniques For CIOs To Use In Order To Secure Both Their IT Department And Their Company

- What CIOs Need To Know In Order To Successfully Manage An IT Department: Decision Making Skills That

Every CIO Needs To Have In Order To Be Able To Make The Right Choices

- How CIOs Can Make Innovation Happen: Tips And Techniques For CIOs To Use In Order To Make Innovation Happen In Their IT Department

IT Manager Skills

- How To Build High Performance IT Teams: Tips And Techniques That IT Managers Can Use In Order To Develop Productive Teams

- Building The Perfect Team: What Staffing Skills Do IT Managers Need?: Tips And Techniques That IT Managers Can Use In Order To Correctly Staff Their Teams

- Secrets Of Effective Leadership For IT Managers: Tips And Techniques That IT Managers Can Use In Order To Develop Leadership Skills

Negotiating

- Exploring How To Get The Deal That You Want In A Negotiation: How To Develop The Skill Of Exploring What Is Possible In A Negotiation In Order To Reach The Best Possible Deal

- Use The Power Of Arguing To Win Your Next Negotiation: How To Develop The Skill Of Effective

Arguing In A Negotiation In Order To Get The Best Possible Outcome

Miscellaneous

- How To Heal A Broken Leg – Fast!: Understanding how to deal with a broken leg in order to start walking again quickly

- How Software Defined Networking (SDN) Is Going To Change Your World Forever: The Revolution In Network Design And How It Affects

Note: See a complete list of books by Dr. Jim Anderson at the back of this book.

Acknowledgements

Any book like this one is the result of years of real-world work experience. In my over 25 years of working for 7 different firms, I have met countless fantastic people and I've been mentored by some truly exceptional ones. Although I've probably forgotten some of the people who made me the person that I am today, here is my attempt to finally give them the recognition that they so truly deserve:

- Thomas P. Anderson
- Art Puett
- Bobbi Marshall
- Bob Boggs

Dr. Jim Anderson

This book is dedicated to my wife Lori. None of this would have been possible without her love and support.

Thanks for the best years of my life (so far)...!

Speaking. Negotiating. Managing. Marketing.

Table Of Contents

YOU ARE THE ONLY PERSON WHO IS RESPONSIBLE FOR MANAGING YOUR CAREER 9

ABOUT THE AUTHOR..11

CHAPTER 1: PRODUCT MANAGER JOB HUNT: DO YOU HAVE THE COVER LETTER COVERED? 16

CHAPTER 2: PRODUCT MANAGER RESUME CREATION: BACK TO THE FUTURE? 20

CHAPTER 3: IS YOUR PRODUCT MANAGER RESUME IPHONE READY? 24

CHAPTER 4: 3 SKILLS THAT MOST PRODUCT MANAGERS ARE MISSING..28

CHAPTER 5: SHOULD PRODUCT MANAGERS CONSIDER GETTING A HYBRID MBA? 32

CHAPTER 6: IS YOUR PRODUCT TEAM'S SILENCE KILLING YOUR PRODUCT? 36

CHAPTER 7: BREAKTHROUGH IN SOLVING THE PROBLEM OF HOW TO EVALUATE A PRODUCT MANAGER 40

CHAPTER 8: NOW WHAT? WHEN PRODUCT MANAGERS MAKE THE WRONG JOB MOVE... 45

CHAPTER 9: 4 THINGS THAT REAL WORLD PRODUCT MANAGERS DO 49

CHAPTER 10: ONLY A PRODUCT MANAGER COULD SCREW UP A JOB CHANGE! 53

CHAPTER 11: GREAT PRODUCT MANAGERS AREN'T AFRAID TO STUMBLE ON THE WAY TO THE TOP 57

CHAPTER 12: PRODUCT MANAGERS NEED TO LEARN HOW TO FAIL.61

You Are The Only Person Who Is Responsible For Managing Your Career

Do you have the perfect product manager job? I'm willing to bet that the answer to that question is probably no. Every product manager job has a certain level of excitement and job satisfaction; however, sometimes we start to get interested in finding our next position. When we start to feel this way, we need remember just exactly how you go about finding your next product manager job.

The first thing that we need to keep in mind is that we're going to need to create a cover letter that does a good job of introducing us and what we can do. Next comes, of course, our resume. This will be where we explain to a hiring manager why we're the right person for the job.

The hunt for your next job may be different the next time that you kick it off. We are now living in the mobile age and what this means for you is that there is a very good chance that the hiring manager will be reviewing your resume on a cell phone or a tablet. Is your resume ready for this type of inspection?

If we want to move our career along at the company that we are currently working for, there is a question about what's going to make us more valuable. One thing to consider is getting an MBA – in fact, a hybrid MBA might be the right choice for a product manager. We also have to realize that the success of our product is what will boost our career so we need to make sure that our team is not being silent about what they are doing.

How to judge the performance of a product manager has always been a challenge. We manage many things, but we control precious few things. There is a new way that has become available that can be used to determine how good of a job a product manager is doing. If we do choose to move on to a new job, we hope that we've made the right selection. However, if we've chosen poorly, what should we do then?

Nobody is perfect and product managers are not perfect either. What we need to understand is that we will occasionally fail. We have to get over our fear of failure and understand that there is a correct way to fail that will allow us to grow as product managers.

For more information on what it takes to be a great product manager, check out my blog, The Accidental Product Manager, at:

www.TheAccidentalPM.com

Good luck!

- Dr. Jim Anderson

About The Author

I must confess that I never set out to be a product manager. When I went to school, I studied Computer Science and thought that I'd get a nice job programming and that would be that. Well, at least part of that plan worked out!

My first job was working for Boeing on their F/A-18 fighter jet program. I spent my days programming fighter jet software in assembly language and I loved it. The U.S. government decided to save some money and went looking for other countries to sell this plane to. This put me into an unfamiliar role: I started to meet with foreign military officials in order to explain what my product did.

Time moved on and so did I. I found myself working for Siemens, the big German telecommunications company. They were making phone switches and selling them to the seven U.S. phone companies. The problem was that the switches were too complicated. Customers couldn't tell the difference between one complicated phone switch from another complicated phone switch.

The Siemens sales folks were in a bind. They didn't know enough about how the switches worked to tell their customers why they should buy them. Siemens reached out into their engineering unit looking for anyone who could help the sales teams out. I put my hand up and overnight I became a product manager.

Since then I've spent over 20 years working as a product manager for both big companies and startups. This has given me an opportunity to do everything that a product manager does many, many times. I know what works as well as what doesn't work.

I now live in Tampa Florida where I spend my time managing my consulting business, Blue Elephant Consulting, teaching college courses at the University of South Florida, and traveling to work with companies like yours to share the knowledge that I have about how product managers can make their product be a success.

I'm always available to answer questions and I can be reached at:

Dr. Jim Anderson
Blue Elephant Consulting
Email: jim@BlueElephantConsulting.com
Facebook: http://goo.gl/1TVoK
Web: **www.BlueElephantConsulting.com**

"Unforgettable communication skills that will set your ideas free…"

Create Products Your Customers Want At A Price That They Are Willing To Pay!

Dr. Jim Anderson is available to provide training and coaching on the two topics that are the most important to product managers everywhere: how do I create the products that my customers want and what should I price them at?

Dr. Anderson believes that in order to both learn and remember what he says, product managers need to laugh. Each one of his speeches is full of fun and humor so that what he says "sticks" with everyone.

Dr. Anderson's Product Management Training Includes:

1. How can you segment your market?
2. What problems are your customers having right now?
3. Which of your customer's problems does your product solve?
4. How much of this problem does your product solve?
5. How much will it cost your customer if they don't fix this problem?

Dr. Jim Anderson presents over 100 speeches per year. To invite Dr. Anderson to speak at your event, contact him at:

Phone: 813-418-6970 or
Email: jim@BlueElephantConsulting.com

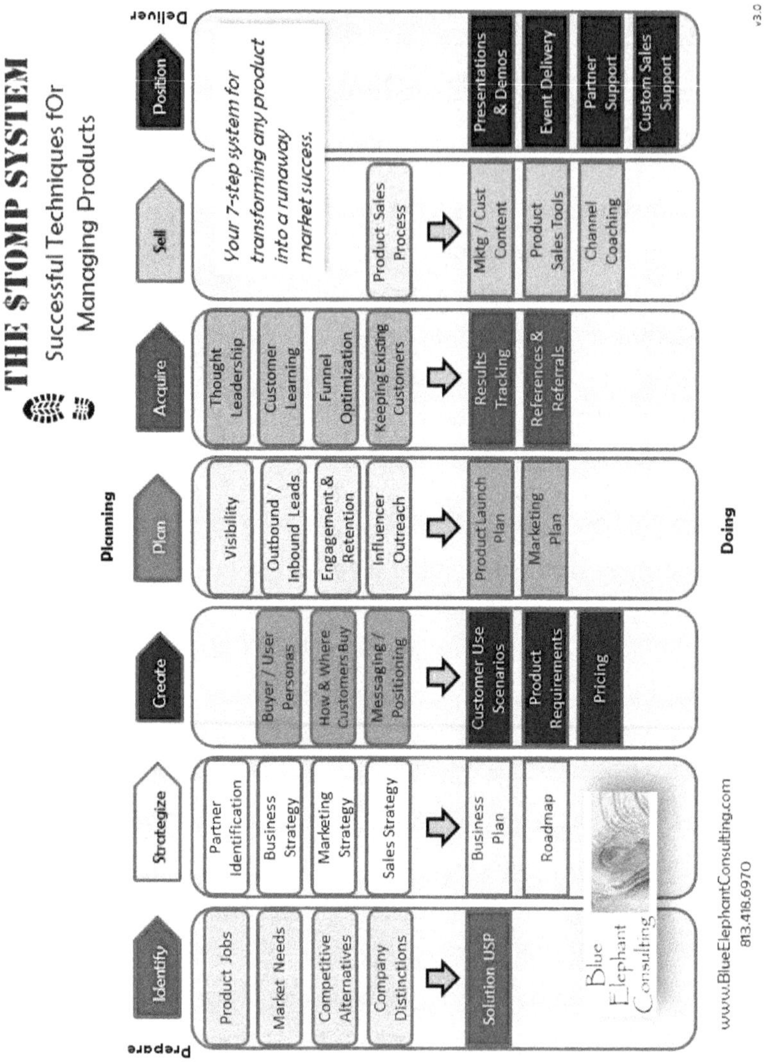

THE $TOMP SYSTEM
Successful Techniques fOr Managing Products

Your 7-step system for transforming any product into a runaway market success.

Prepare

- **Identify**: Product Jobs, Market Needs, Competitive Alternatives, Company Distinctions ⇒ Solution USP
- **Strategize**: Partner Identification, Business Strategy, Marketing Strategy, Sales Strategy ⇒ Business Plan, Roadmap

Planning

- **Create**: Buyer / User Personas, How & Where Customers Buy, Messaging / Positioning ⇒ Customer Use Scenarios, Product Requirements, Pricing
- **Plan**: Visibility, Outbound / Inbound Leads, Engagement & Retention, Influencer Outreach ⇒ Product Launch Plan, Marketing Plan

Doing

- **Acquire**: Thought Leadership, Customer Learning, Funnel Optimization, Keeping Existing Customers ⇒ Results Tracking, References & Referrals
- **Sell**: Product Sales Process ⇒ Mktg / Cust Content, Product Sales Tools, Channel Coaching

Deliver

- **Position**: Presentations & Demos, Event Delivery, Partner Support, Custom Sales Support

www.BlueElephantConsulting.com
813.418.6970

v3.0

The **$TOMP** product management system has been created by **Blue Elephant Consulting** to help product managers know what to do and when to do it in order for a product to be successful.

Chapter 1

Product Manager Job Hunt: Do You Have The Cover Letter Covered?

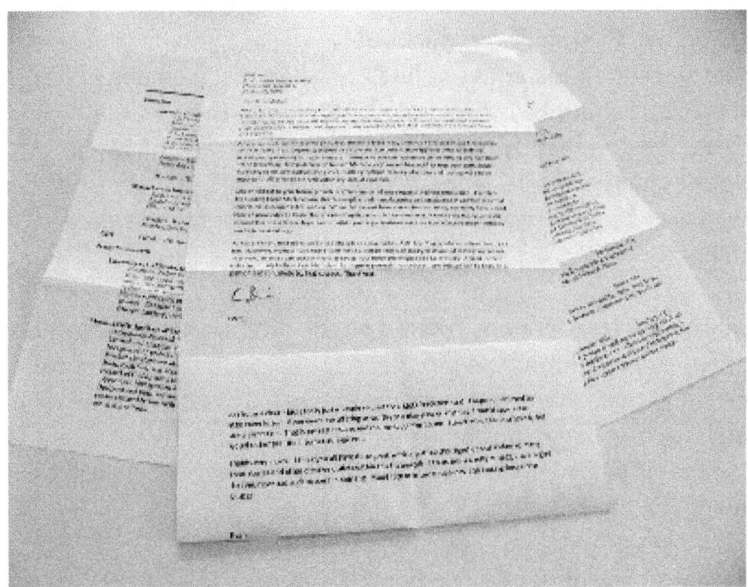

Chapter 1: Product Manager Job Hunt: Do You Have The Cover Letter Covered?

When it comes time for you to go looking for your next Product Management job you'll be facing **a major decision**. I'm not talking about if you should use online resume services or go with a headhunter. I'm not even talking about if creating a more technical or a more business-focused resume is going to land you that next job. I'm talking about something even bigger – the question of whether or not you should create a cover letter when you send someone your resume.

The Purpose Of A Cover Letter For A Product Manager

The product managers that I've been talking with seem to be split down the middle on this issue. Many of them have decided that since their resumes are just going to get scanned in and then checked for keywords, why bother with the cover letter? Others realize that by including a cover letter **they have a better chance** of setting themselves apart from everyone else who may be applying for the job and that's got to be a good thing.

All cover letters are not created equal. Product managers who are applying for multiple jobs need to realize that a cover letter can help them stand out from the crowd. Each letter needs to be both brief (keep it short!) and custom tailored to both the job that is being applied to as well as the employer who will be doing the hiring.

Rarely do any of us grow up hoping to become a product manager. We often just happen into this profession. **This is something that may need to be explained in your cover letter.**

How A Product Manager Can Customize A Cover Letter

In order to make your cover letter read like it was written for the person who is reading it (and not like you copied it out of some book), **you're going to have to customize it**. It turns out that this really is not all that hard to do.

An easy way to customize a cover letter is to **make a reference to the employer's products or services**. Another way is to make a reference to some information that they have on their web site such as their latest press release. If neither of these seem appropriate, then you can do some research and make a reference to something that is going on in their industry.

Your ultimate goal here is to take the time to customize your cover letter **to support the position that you are applying for**. This means that in the limited space provided you should take the time to show how the work that you've done in the past has prepared you for this position better than anyone else out there.

The real power of a cover letter is that it allows you to put all of your work experience **into context** for the person who is reading it – you get to explain why you are the best candidate for the job.

What A Product Manager Should NOT Put Into A Cover Letter

Right off the bat I hope that we can agree that any obvious errors such as misspellings or grammatical mistakes in your cover letter will count against you. These **simple-to-avoid errors** show sloppiness and lack of attention to detail on your part. This is why you always want to get someone else to read over your cover letter before you send it off.

Form cover letters are also a big no-no. What product managers seem to forget is that the people who will be reading our cover letters do this for a living. That means that they've probably seen just about every form cover letter out there. Take the time to write a custom cover letter!

Once you've got one cover letter written, **you might be tempted to reuse it**. Don't! Since much of the job application process has been digitized these days, using the same cover letter to apply for more than one position will be found out quickly and you'll be out of the running.

One final thought, although much has been written about the power of a **hand-written letter** that is delivered by the postal service, it turns out that recruiters just like the rest of us live and die by email. If your cover letter can't be forwarded to the hiring manager by the recruiter, then it loses much of its power.

What All Of This Means For You.

Applying for a new product management job can be **a nerve racking experience**. In order to boost your odds of success, take the time to create a cover letter to send along with your resume.

Make sure that you create **a custom cover letter** that matches the position that you are applying for. Spelling errors or trying to use a form cover letter will end up counting against you.

Getting your next job is often a **numbers game**: you've got to be in the right place at the right time. If a well-done cover letter can help your chances of getting the job, then I say go for it…!

Chapter 2

Product Manager Resume Creation: Back To The Future?

Chapter 2: Product Manager Resume Creation: Back To The Future?

It is the time of year that a product manager's thoughts turn to … searching for a new job? During the global recession, things were so bad for so long that most product managers were just trying to hold on to the jobs that they already had. Now that things appear to be slowly getting better, the calls from the recruiters are starting to ring once again. **Will you be ready when you get a call?**

It's All About Your Resume

Sure, sure – we live in the all-digital 21st Century where the old ways of getting your next job are long gone and now candidates are **automatically selected by computers** that spend their days trolling Facebook and LinkedIn. Well, not quite.

It turns out that how you present your product manager experience in a resume **still matters** because eventually once you get past the robots, real live humans read the things. How you go about structuring your resume can have a significant impact on how well it works for you (or doesn't).

Perhaps we should spend a moment or two talking about **how to create a resume that will do the job for you.**

Which Way Should Your Resume Be Looking?

Phyllis Korkki over at the New York Times has done some digging into just what makes a resume work and she's come up with some interesting findings. The first thing that all product managers should realize is that a resume is first and foremost a way to market yourself – it's your very own **personal product brochure.**

That being said, what your resume should really be doing is telling the reader **what you are capable of doing in the future** – not focusing on what you've done in the past. This means that you should take the time to figure out what kind of job you want to have in the future, and then make sure that your resume focuses on those jobs & skills that have prepared you for the future job that you want.

Here's an important point: your resume is not designed to be **your personal work autobiography**. What this means is that you really don't have to list every job that you've ever had. In fact, anything that is over 15 years old should get very little space or perhaps should be dropped all together...

It's your **most recent jobs** that will count the most when you are searching for your next job. This means that you are going to want to quantify what you've been able to accomplish in those jobs as much as possible – this is a good way to use your precious resume real estate.

Make It Easy To Hire You

I'm always amazed at how often I see product manager's resumes that make me work to find the answers to my questions. When you are submitting a resume for a specific job, be sure to **customize it** so that it contains key words that have to do with that job as well as inserting some terms from the job description that were used to define the job. This makes it easier for the reader to understand how your experience relates to the job that they are trying to fill.

What All Of This Means For You

In order to land your next job, there are a lot of things that have to go just right. You need to discover that someone has a product manager opening, you've got to look good to them both on paper and in person, and they need to end up picking you. Can this happen – yes. However, **your resume can be a key tool** for making it happen quicker rather than later.

You've got to make sure that your product manager resume is **saying the right things**: focus on telling the story about how your past jobs have prepared you for the job that you are now looking for. Although we are often proud of all of the jobs that we've had, it's not necessary to list them all on your resume, especially if they happened a long time ago.

Resumes still do count even in this day and age. Product managers who take the time to create a resume that does a good job of marketing what they have to offer will be able to find their next job faster than everyone else.

Chapter 3

Is Your Product Manager Resume iPhone Ready?

Chapter 3: Is Your Product Manager Resume iPhone Ready?

When you go hunting for your next Product Manager job (and it may be sooner than later), **will your resume be up to the job?** Come to think of it, when was the last time you dusted off and updated your resume? Do you still have that quaint "objective statement" or "career goal" hanging out at the top? If so, you may be in for a shock – that's not going to be the best use of resume real estate when it's being reviewed on the hiring manager's iPhone…

The Need For A New Resume

Parting is such sweet sorrow… or so the classic line goes. Look, when did you first create your product manager resume? A while ago? Even if it was only a couple of years ago, **the world has changed dramatically since then** and it's time that you (and your resume) kept up with it. It's time to say goodbye to your old style resume.

About that "objective statement" up at the top – **ditch it**. The next company that will be hiring you really doesn't care about what you are looking for. Instead, they are facing pain right now and they are looking for someone whom they can hire to come in and make that pain go away. That's what really matters.

This means that we're going to have to make some changes to your current resume. **Prepare to get out the sharp knife.**

Length

How long is too long? How long is too short? This rule of thumb has not changed even in the 21st Century – **a resume should be two pages max**. In fact, it's really only the first 25% that you can count on a hiring manager reading so that's where you've got to really shine.

If you've had some amazing product management experiences that you think would really help your case, then feel free to include them – **as an addendum**. This extra stuff can be anywhere from 4-12 pages long; however, remember that there is no guarantee that anyone is going to read it.

Skills

Are you the world's best Cobol / Fortran / Java programmer? Drop it. Look, you're going for a product management job and it's really your leadership and project management skills that are going to get you the job – **not your programming chops**. Use your limited resume real estate to explain how your product management skills have made your past products successful.

Skip The History Lesson

A resume is designed to tell your next employer about how you'll perform in the workplace. This means that pretty much anything that does not have to do with the workplace **should be dropped**. This list will include civic accomplishments, professional associations that you belong to, charity work, etc. Use the freed up space to provide more details about your most recent job and how it relates to the job that you are applying for.

Say No To Descriptions, Yes To Accomplishments

I must confess that this has been a mistake that I've made in the past and I found it hard to stop doing it. Instead of providing your work biography by listing every single job you've ever had, use the space instead to **list your accomplishments**. Ultimately this is what your future employer really cares about. Don't worry about all of those "title only" promotions that you've gotten over the years, instead just focus on the products that you've managed and the challenges that you've mastered.

What All Of This Means For You

Everyone has a resume. However, not everyone has a resume that will work for them. In this day and age of everyone having too much to do and too little time to do it in, you're going to need to shape your resume **to be scanned quickly on your future boss' iPhone** as he/she dashes off to their next meeting.

What this means is that you're going to have to **cut to the bone** and get rid of everything that doesn't pertain to how you would do in your next position. Detailing what you've accomplished in your most recent product management positions is what that iPhone scanning hiring manager is going to be looking for.

Take the time to craft a new resume that is tailored to be read quickly in digital form and **you'll be one step ahead of everyone else** who is applying for the same job. If you make it easy for them to see why you are the perfect fit for the job, then you've just shown them why you're the product manager that they need to hire…

Chapter 4

3 Skills That Most Product Managers Are Missing

Chapter 4: 3 Skills That Most Product Managers Are Missing

I'm guessing that you wouldn't go to work naked. Then why-oh-why are heading off to your product management job when you don't have all of the skills that you'll need to do the job correctly?

I'm not sure if this is going to make you feel any better, but it turns out that most product managers are showing up for work only partially dressed when you consider **what skills they are missing**. Maybe we'd better have a talk about this...

Can You Communicate?

All too often, we marketing folks assume that good communication skills simply means that you have the ability to get up in front of a group of people and **deliver a speech** without bursting into flames. Yes, this is good skill to have, but a product manager has to have more.

Remember, communication is **a two-way street** and not only does a product manager need to be able to tell others what to do, but you are also going to have to be able to listen to what others are telling you.

No, we're not talking about having the ability to sit there and listen when someone else is talking to you just waiting for them to pause so that you can start talking again. Instead, a product manager needs to be able to listen, process what has been said, and then **ask good, pointed questions** that will help get to the bottom of any discussion.

Just to round things out, a product manager also needs to have the communication skill that will allow them to **"close" a discussion**. This is when you ask a final question and then have the strength to keep your mouth closed and allow the other person to provide an answer. This is how you wrap things up cleanly.

Promote, Promote, Promote!

All too often product managers seem to have a "build it and they will come" sort of attitude. They believe that if they do a good job then the rest of the company will realize it and **their value to the company will increase**. Sorry, it doesn't work that way.

What product managers need to be doing is **constantly promoting** both themselves and their product. Now you have to be careful here, note that I didn't say "bragging". The difference is subtle, but important.

One way that a product manager can show the value of both his position as well as the value that his / her product brings to the company is to become the **thought leader** on all things about the market that the product addresses. By researching what drives the market and then taking the time to educate the rest of the company about what customers are really looking for, both the product manager and their product will become recognized as a valuable resource.

Make A Friend (or Two)

Within the world of marketing, there is often **a "loner" attitude** that many of us hold: I can do it all by myself. As a product manager, you need to stop thinking this way and start making as many contacts as you can.

A product manager is only as strong as his / her network and that means taking the time to **develop real relationships** with as many people as possible. Not all product managers have this skill.

What All Of This Means For You

If you really want to become a successful product manager, **you've got some work to do**. There are a set of skills that you'll need to develop in order to ensure that both your career and your product get the kind of positive attention that you both deserve.

In order to become a successful product manager, you're going to have to have the ability to be **a good two-way communicator**. You'll have to learn to spend your time tirelessly promoting both your product's value as well as your own value to the company. Finally, you are going to have to get good at that critical job skill: networking.

None of these three skills are impossible to do. However, the key to being a successful product manager is to get good at **doing all three at the same time**...!

Chapter 5

Should Product Managers Consider Getting A Hybrid MBA?

Chapter 5: Should Product Managers Consider Getting A Hybrid MBA?

Product Managers have long struggled with the idea of getting an MBA. Sure, it seems like a good idea, but who has the time or the energy to haul yourself off to some college campus several times a week to attend classes. There are those "online" universities that let you get an MBA online, but they still seem just a big shady. Isn't there another way to get the results that you want?

Say Hello To The Hybrid MBA

Business schools have heard the cries of product managers (and others) and they have responded by creating a new product for them: the hybrid MBA. This type of MBA involves limited time on campus and a lot of time online.

The target market for this type of MBA are students who want to get a degree, but who simply either don't have the time or the ability to make it to campus several times a week. Schools like to offer these programs because they are generally less costly for the school because the students in the program are on campus less often.

It's important to note that these hybrid MBA programs generally end up costing the student roughly the same as they would pay to attend a traditional full-time MBA program on campus. However, the good news is that the courses will be taught by the same professors who teach the full-time program.

One of the main ways that students learn in a traditional MBA program is by working in teams on projects. The hybrid programs use the same concept, the only difference is that the students interact via either conference calls or by using Skype.

Similar Yet Different

Let's be frank here, a hybrid MBA program is not the same as an on-campus MBA program. There are some key differences that any product manager needs to be aware of before starting one of these programs.

One of the nice differences between hybrid and in-person programs is that it's often easier to get into the hybrid program – entrance requirements are lower. Some don't even require that you take the traditional gatekeeper exam: the GMAT.

You won't get a chance to become as well-rounded as you might like. Since not all MBA classes will be part of the hybrid program, some of the elective courses that you might have taken to broaden your skills won't be available to you.

Some of the most important parts of any MBA program are the access to professors that it gives you along with the ability to make use of on-campus resources (think "career services"). Simply because you're not going to be there as much as full-time students, you won't be able to tap into these two resources as much as you might like to.

Another key part of any MBA program is the network that you build with your fellow students. Once again, this can be hard to do in a hybrid MBA program since you won't be working with them shoulder to shoulder.

Who Do These Hybrid MBA Programs Work Best For?

So all of that brings up a good point: what type of student does a hybrid MBA program work best for? People involved with the programs say that they work well for internationally based professionals who can't take two years off of their careers to spend on campus.

Additionally, if you are working for a company and you'd really like to position yourself for a future international assignment, a hybrid MBA might be your ticket to doing so. You'll be able to keep working while you get the degree that will open doors to future assignments at the same time.

What All Of This Means For You

Whether or not to spend the time and money to get an MBA is a personal decision that every product manager has to wrestle with at some point in time. One of the biggest obstacles to getting this type of degree is the time and effort that going to campus for classes may pose.

The arrival of the hybrid MBA may solve this problem for some product managers. Trips to campus are minimized. However, it may not be the best way for product managers who have a technical background to pick up the team skills and soft skills that they'll need in their future career.

If you do decide to get an MBA, you now have one more option for how you actually go about getting it. You'll have to make the decision as to how important it is to learn in a classroom or learn online. More knowledge is always good for you, no matter how you get it!

Chapter 6

Is Your Product Team's Silence Killing Your Product?

Chapter 6: Is Your Product Team's Silence Killing Your Product?

It turns out that **a Product Manager really doesn't do all that much**. I mean, they don't actually create the product and they don't actually sell the thing now do they? Sorta makes you wonder just exactly they do do? It turns out that most of a Product Manager's time is spent doing scary stuff, like managing people and getting them to work together in order to get a product created and out the door…

Why Silence Is NOT Golden

So here's an interesting thought: if one of your primary jobs as a Product Manager is to do a good job of managing all of the people who work on your product, then how are you going to be able to tell **if you are doing a good job?** One way that might come to mind right off the bat is if you don't hear any complaints than certainly you must be doing a good job, right?

It turns out that Dr. James Detert, a researcher at Cornell, and a team have been looking into **what workers do and don't tell the people that they are working with**. The results (and the reasons for them) just might surprise you. Here are four common myths that every Product Manager should know are not true.

Myth: Women Are Less Likely To Speak Up

Most Product Managers believe that women and non-professional workers are more likely to **NOT speak up** simply because they think that it will either harm their career or just isn't worth the effort. I must confess that I believed this myth.

It turns out that this just isn't so. Based on studies that were done by Dr. Detert and his team, it turns out that women and non-professional workers are **just as likely as professional men to speak up in the workplace**. In fact, the researchers have shown that your gender, level of education, and your level of income have no bearing on the probability that you'll express your opinions at work.

Myth: Talkers Tell All

Product Managers who are getting a lot of feedback from their product team may **start to feel confidant** that they are in touch with everything that is going on. I mean come on, if your team is talking to you then they've got to be telling you everything, right?

Sorry, once again it turns out that this is not the case. In studies that were done by the researchers it turned out that almost half of the workers polled said that **they hold back**. The reasons varied, but the most common causes of team members holding their tongues were when they thought it wouldn't do any good or when they thought it might harm their career.

Myth: Safety First

Product Managers who have a problem with their staff not talking to them may wonder why. A natural first assumption is that their product team for some reason **doesn't feel safe doing so**. For some reason, the thinking goes, they believe that speaking up about an issue will come back to haunt them.

Well guess what, the reason that your staff might not be talking to you is actually **much more boring than that**. The number one reason that staff won't tell a product manager what's really going on is, drum roll please, simply because they are too busy – they don't want to waste their time. Ouch, that hurts!

Myth: Only The Big Issues Are Scary

Finally, you would assume that it would be **the big issues** that would cause product team members to hold back. You know, things that involve actual crimes or unethical things. Oops, once again you'd be wrong.

The researchers found that members of a product team **will not speak up on even the smallest issues**. Unfortunately these are the very issues that a Product Manager needs to hear about if he / she wants to improve how their product can help the company operate.

What All Of This Means For You

The product specific part of being a Product Manager is probably easier than **the people part**. However, you are going to have to be good at both if you want to be a successful Product Manager.

One of the most important things that you'll need to realize is that your best way of **identifying issues** within the product team is to get your staff to tell you about them. Not hearing about issues doesn't mean that they don't exist. We've pointed out four myths that can lead a Product Manager to make the wrong conclusions.

Now that you know that silence doesn't necessarily mean that you don't have any problems, **you are ready to take the next step**. This means that you've got to go out and form real relationships with your product team so that you'll be able to tell when they are holding back – and then you'll know that it's time to dig deeper!

Chapter 7

Breakthrough In Solving The Problem Of How To Evaluate A Product Manager

Chapter 7: Breakthrough In Solving The Problem Of How To Evaluate A Product Manager

Oh do I have a tasty dilemma for you this time around! I've been working with one of my clients who is setting up a brand new product management department. He's faced with a challenge that you'd think would be more common than it appears to be: just how should you **evaluate the job that a product manager is doing?**

Product Managers Are Not Project Managers

The newly minted manager of product managers was struggling. It was the beginning of the year and one of the things that he had to do on his list of tasks was to set up **annual goals** for his team.

This manager was coming from a project management background. In his first pass at creating goals for his team this training really came across: **all of the goals had to do with meeting dates**. Clearly there's more to being a product manager than this.

He was facing a revolt from his product management team when I was brought in to see if I could broker a solution to this problem. The manager had a valid need to be able to manage his product managers, but they also had a reasonable expectation that they would be measured **based on what a product manager does**, not on what a project manager does.

Say Hello To The Puppet Master

I stated out by having a talk with the manager who was trying to come up with the goals. It turned out that he really didn't have a clear understanding of **what product managers do**. In a nutshell, he viewed product managers as sort of a "super project manager". The only problem with this is that the company had project managers who worked on every product's team. Clearly there had to be something different in what these two groups of employees were doing.

I then took some time and met with the product managers themselves. It turns out that they were all busy **doing exactly what you would expect a product manager to be doing**: studying markets, guiding product developers, and putting out fires.

After having collected all of the available information, I brought the manager and his team back together. I started this meeting out by taking the time to explain to the manager **the role that product managers played in his company**.

Right or wrong, I used the analogy of **a puppet master** (you know, those old-time puppeteers who controlled the puppets by pulling on strings connected to their hands and feet). I pointed out to him that the role of the product manager was not so much to do things, but rather to make sure that things got done. Product managers are like information hubs. They ensure that the right information gets to the right person at the right time so that they can accomplish a task.

The difference between a product manager and a project manager can be murky at times. However, I pointed out that if the product manager told the project manager **to build a 3-wheeled car**, the project manager would make sure that the car got built on time and on budget. However, when the car flopped in the marketplace, it would be the product manager's fault because he had said that a 3-wheeled car was what the world needed.

A New Way To Evaluate Product Managers

What was needed here was **a new way to evaluate product managers**. Others have discussed this topic and they've focused on getting the product's requirements correct. I think that this is important; however, the product manager's job does not end there.

What I told the manager and his team was that a much better way to evaluate product managers is to focus on **the four areas that a product manager actually controls**. These all have to do with the up-front work of determining what product to create, creating the product, and then ensuring that the product is a success once it's been made.

The four areas include: knowledge of the market, providing a well understood business strategy, empowering the company with product tactics, and directing the creation of product related content. Each one of these areas has plenty of room for **individual performance metrics** to be created that can be used to evaluate how well a product manager is doing his / her job.

What All Of This Means For You

Product managers, just like every other employee in a company, **need to be evaluated** in order to determine if they are doing a good job. The problem is that nobody really seems to have come up with a good way of doing this.

Product managers are not project managers. This means that the traditional management metrics of delivering a product on a given date and keeping it on budget, don't really seem to apply to product managers.

What a product manager does is pretty much all **"behind the scenes"**. We deal in relationships as we get people to do different things at different times. We are an information hub that provides the right information to the right people at the right time.

A much better way to **evaluate product managers** is to focus on the four areas that a product manager actually controls: knowledge of the market, providing a well understood business strategy, empowering the company with product tactics, and directing the creation of product related content.

The performance of a product manager can be measured. However, you need to be very careful to do it in terms of **what a product manager does**, not what a project manager does. Once you establish the proper metrics to measure your product manager by, you'll be able to determine just how successful your products are going to be.

Chapter 8

Now What? When Product Managers Make The Wrong Job Move...

Chapter 8: Now What? When Product Managers Make The Wrong Job Move...

Sure you did all of the research, you talked with all of the right people, shucks you even followed up on every Google link that you could find on the company that you were thinking about going to work for before making the jump. However, now that you've made the jump you are finding out that perhaps **you've made a mistake**. Now what do you do?

How Did This Happen?

Product managers are supposed to be smart people, how come we can end up making mistakes when it comes time to switch jobs? The good news is that we are smart; however, what can happen is that we can find ourselves under a great deal of pressure and this can **adversely affect how we make decisions**.

One such type of pressure is mental pressure – **how do we see ourselves**? When we are considering making a job change, we tend to make up our minds about how we think the next job is going to be and then we only pay attention to the information that we encounter that confirms this view. Researchers call this thinking "confirmation bias".

In order to counter this kind of thinking we need to be constantly asking ourselves one question: **what happens if I am wrong?** Only by doing this will you be able to make yourself aware of information that might not fit the way that you want the world to be.

Another type of pressure you need to deal with when you are considering changing jobs is social pressure. This is most often evident when you have become so unhappy with your current job that **you'd almost rather be anywhere else**.

Far too often these types of situations could be dealt with if you would only find the courage to sit down and **talk things over with someone at your current company**. However, all too often we are so resistant to having this kind of discussion that we're willing to leave the firm and run to a new job.

Finally, the ever present specter of time pressure is always a factor when it comes to considering moving to a new job. When we don't feel that we have very much time to make a decision, what happens is that **we end up hastily making a bad decision**.

The lack of time forces us to **focus on the short-term gains** that we'll make by switching jobs. What happens is that we forget to take a look at the long-term impacts of making the switch. A good way of countering this tendency is to ask yourself questions such as "if the salaries & benefits were the same, would I make the job switch?"

What Do You Do Now?

Despite having taken the time to carefully consider all of the issues and to try to counter the pressures that will be driving your decision, sometimes we still end up making poor job change choices. The question then comes up: **what should we do now?**

The experts all agree on the answer to this one. You need to **cut your losses** and move on once again. However, this time around you need to do a better job. Don't just flee a bad job and jump yet again into another poor position. Take the time to understand why you made a bad job change decision and make sure that you don't repeat this mistake.

Ultimately the best way to protect yourself from making another bad career decision is to **become more self-aware**. You want to be able to understand your strengths and weaknesses so that you can evaluate your next job opportunity in a way that will reveal if it is really the right career move for you.

What All Of This Means For You

Despite our best efforts, sometimes we make mistakes when we are **switching product management jobs**. There can be a number of different reasons that we make this kind of mistake but more often than not they all come back to the different types of pressures that we are under: mental, social, or time.

If you find yourself having made the wrong choice in switching jobs, your next step is very clear. You need to cut your losses and **move on to your next job**. You need to be careful and make sure that you leave your new job carefully so that it doesn't look like you are running away from it.

None of us is perfect – we all have the ability to make the wrong decision at some point in time. What can make us a great product manager is the ability to **be aware that we've made a poor decision** and then the ability to react and make the right decision.

Chapter 9

4 Things That Real World Product Managers Do

Chapter 9: 4 Things That Real World Product Managers Do

What do product managers **really spend their time doing**? We like to talk about all of the things that a product manager should be spending their time doing – boldly defining new products and clearly laying out markets to go after. However, the day-to-day reality of being a product manager can be quite different. The folks over at Pragmatic Marketing have just released their annual product manager survey and it contains some interesting points…

Roadmaps

If ever there was a part of a product that a product manager should own, the roadmap is it. Just to make sure that we're all on the same page here, **a product roadmap** lays out the changes and enhancements that are planned for your product in the future. You get to define the future: is it just this month, this year, or do you go out for 5 years?

Although the product manager should own the product's roadmap, this is not always an easy thing to do. Development teams have been known to want to **play a big role** in saying what shows up in the product and when it shows up.

The reason that this is the wrong way to handle things is that for your product to be successful, it really needs to be **your customers** who are defining in what order (and when) features are introduced. Who owns the roadmap can be the source of many battles within the firm.

Requirements

When people ask me what skills a product manager needs to have, at the top of my list is **the ability to communicate clearly**. Nowhere is this more evident than when it comes to product requirements.

Product managers **own the requirements for their products**. Normally, the creation of product requirements is not something that people fight over. I mean, who really wants to do all of that writing?

The key skill that a product manager needs to have is the ability to both clearly and succinctly express **what the product needs to be able to do**. This has to be done for multiple simultaneous audiences: the sales teams need to be able to read it and understand what's coming and the development teams need to be able to read it and understand what they need to do.

Market Problems

In a world without problems, there probably wouldn't be much of a need for product managers. Thankfully there are a lot of problems out there! I'm not sure if "problems" is really the right word to use here, I think that **"changes"** might be closer to the mark…

When we create and launch a product, we do so in a market that has **certain characteristics**: we know who our customers are and we know who we are competing against. From that moment on everything changes.

As things change, it is the responsibility of the product manager to **change with it**. We need to adapt our products, our marketing message, and perhaps even our pricing to deal with the new realities as they show up.

Positioning

What does your product do? Who does it do it for it? Why should your customers choose your product over somebody else's? These are all **great questions** and if you don't have a solid answer for each of them, things are not looking good for your product.

Knowing how you want people to view your product against all of their other options is a key point that product managers have to take care of. This higher level ability to **"see" your product** as the market does is very important.

Since we are dealing with an ever changing market, your product positioning **will always be changing also**. This means that as a product manager you need to always be "looking" at your product and making marketing adjustments to it.

What All Of This Means For You

It's not easy being a product manager. There is no such thing as a product that just **"runs on auto pilot"**. Instead, every day we need to be making adjustments to both our products and how we market them in order to ensure that they will be successful.

A recent survey shows that product managers spend a lot of their time working on **four main tasks**. These tasks are: creating roadmaps, defining requirements, dealing with market "problems", and ensuring that their products are properly positioned.

If we can master these activities, then we'll have the core of what it means to be **a great product manager** taken care of. That being said, it's not easy being a product manager; however, at least now you know what's required!

Chapter 10

Only A Product Manager Could Screw Up A Job Change!

Chapter 10: Only A Product Manager Could Screw Up A Job Change!

The global economy is roaring back again and it sure seems like everyone is starting to take stock of their job and decide if they want to stay where they are or **move on to greener pastures**. Product managers are no exception. Perhaps you've grown as far as you can or perhaps you feel that you've done everything that you're going to be allowed to do where you are at. If you are thinking about moving on, you had better be careful that you don't screw up your job change…

Failing To Do Enough Research On Where You Are Going

Considering the fact that doing research, collecting data, and then making the best possible decision is such **a key part of the job of being a product manager**, you'd think that we'd all do this well when it comes to looking for our next job. Well, guess again.

The folks who know such things, search consultants, say that product managers are dropping the ball in several areas. The first is that they don't do a good job of **sizing up the market for their skills**. What this means is that product managers don't have valid assumptions for how long it's going to take to find their next job.

Next, product managers somewhat surprisingly don't do a good job of checking out the financial health of the company that they are thinking about jumping to. Sure they may check out the salary, but not **the bottom line situation**.

Additionally, the culture of the new company is **rarely considered**. If a product manager is coming in from a freewheeling Silicon Valley company and is considering going to work for a 100-year old insurance firm, culture becomes a big deal.

Finally, all too often product managers assume that they are getting what's being advertised – that **the job title matches the job**. Just because the new company calls the job "product manager" does not mean that you'll have the same level of control that you had in your old job.

Going When They Show You The Money

Hey, I like money, you like money. However, as hard as it is for both of us to understand, you can't leave one job and go to another just because the new job pays more. **This is a sure recipe for disaster**.

When product managers were asked to rank what they were looking for in a new job, pay came in at the fourth or fifth place on the list. However, all too often product managers bump this factor up to first place **when it comes time to make a decision** — bad move.

Deciding To Go "From" Rather Than "To"

Just like everyone else out there, product managers can become **dissatisfied with their jobs**. When this happens, they can start to make poor career decisions.

When a product manager decides to switch jobs, it should be **a carefully planned career move**. However, if they are really upset with their current position, then all too often it becomes just a desperate jump to the nearest lifeboat. Since this often happens with little or no serious research into the firm that the product manager is fleeing to, these new positions rarely last for long.

As a product manager bounces from firm to firm, you can quickly develop a reputation as **a job hopper** and it will become that much harder to get your next job. No matter how bad your current job is, take the time to plan out what your next career step should be before you do anything.

What All Of This Means For You

Product managers are like everyone else: when the opportunity to move to a new job comes along, they can decide to make the jump for all of the wrong reasons. If you are aware of the most common mistakes that other product managers have made, then you'll have a chance to avoid them.

The mistakes that product managers make are easily avoidable. The most common mistakes include not doing enough research on the company that they'll be joining, being seduced by an offer of more money, and focusing on leaving the firm where they are and not taking a careful look at just exactly where they'll be going.

Ultimately, being aware of the most common mistakes that product managers make is the first step in avoiding them. You can switch jobs smoothly and end up in a better place, just make sure that you're switching for all the right reasons!

Chapter 11

Great Product Managers Aren't Afraid To Stumble On The Way To The Top

Chapter 11: Great Product Managers Aren't Afraid To Stumble On The Way To The Top

A quick question for you: **are you afraid to fail?** Would you be willing to take on responsibility for a product that might not be a success? I'm willing to bet that a lot of us would say "no" – our company's product managers who are perfect are rewarded while product managers who fail are kicked to the curb. Nowhere on the product manager job description is there a place where you can brag about how many times you've failed. However, I'm going to tell you that you're wrong – get ready to fail if you want to succeed.

How To Kill Your Product Management Career

In your job right now, what would happen to you if you failed? If the account manager and business development manager for your product didn't get to you first, then that end-of-year review would still be a tough one to sit through, right? Let's face it, failure is not something that is rewarded in our workplace and in fact it's something that **we all actively avoid** if we possibly can.

However, maybe we're just setting ourselves up for a much bigger career disaster. Can we all admit that **the world as we know it is changing**? Can you remember watching old-time movies where the hero would get a job at a company and then spend his or her entire career working there? We all know that those days are long gone.

Something else is changing also: our jobs. The job that you had when you started working may already be gone. The one that you're doing right now probably won't exist in what, 2, maybe 3 years from now. This all means that **you are going to have to change** and change involves risk and along with risk comes the very real possibility that you are going to fail.

How To Become A Success By Failing

Well, that failing stuff doesn't sound like it's going to be any fun. But wait, **has anyone else ever failed?** Turns out that yes, in fact most successful people can look at their past and point to failures that helped them to get to where they are now.

The poster child for this kind of "good failure" would be Howard Schultz – the guy who founded **the Starbucks chain of coffee shops**. We all know and love the Starbucks store today, but when Howard first started it he really blew it. There were no chairs, he played lots of opera music, and his menu was in Italian. Clearly he realized that he had failed, quickly adjusted, and went on to become a big success.

You can do the same. Failure is actually a part of your product's overall strategic management. You need to **learn to make lots of small bets**. Some of these bets will pay off, and some won't. It's through what you learn from the failures that you'll be able to make tiny changes to your approach and try, try again.

If we keep doing things the same way that we've always been doing them, then we will eventually stagnate and then **we'll go into decline**. However, if you have the courage to start to fail and to learn from those failures, then the future contains limitless possibilities for both you and your career.

What All Of This Means For You

Product managers who are afraid to fail **will never become a true success**. Oh sure, they may do ok for a few years, but when things get really rough, they'll wash out.

If you are willing to adjust how you view failure, **your career can take off**. Sorry, there's still no place on a product manager resume to proudly list your failures. However, if you can start to look at failures as being simply being learning experiences that are not be feared, but they are to be used to become a better product manager then you'll be able to grow and become better at what you do.

No, you can't be an idiot about this and do silly things that cause your product to fail, but if you try your hardest and your product still fails than **you will have learned what doesn't work**. The big deal is that it takes courage for you to be able to do this.

Product managers who are a success have to had failures in their past. It's from the forge of failure that the steel of success is formed. Learn how to make small bets so that **you can learn what works** and what doesn't. Do this well and you'll become a successful product manager.

Chapter 12

Product Managers Need To Learn How To Fail

Chapter 12: Product Managers Need To Learn How To Fail

How do you feel about failing at something? I'm willing to bet that you are just like the rest of us in that **you HATE to fail**. It turns out that if indeed this is the way that you feel, then perhaps you've been missing out on some great learning opportunities. Maybe I should explain myself...

Your Brain On Failure

Failure should probably be a part of the product development definition. Something that most of us have never spent any time thinking about is just **exactly how we react to failure when it hits us**. More importantly, how our brains react to failure when it shows up. Jonah Lehrer has been looking into this and has made some interesting discoveries.

It turns out that when we fail, two very important things go on inside of our heads. The first is that something called **error-related negativity (ERN)** which is triggered immediately after we realize that something that we've done has failed. We're talking about a signal that shows up 50 milliseconds after the realization that we've failed and there's not a darn thing that you can do about it – it's pretty much involuntary.

However, that's not all. There is another signal that our brain gets about 100-500 milliseconds after we realize that we've failed. This signal is called the **error positivity (Pe)** . We have some control over this signal: it happens when we start to pay attention to our failure and we spend time thinking about the results that have been produced.

The really smart scientists who study such things tell us that product managers who are able to have **a large initial ERN**

signal and a more constant Pe signal are the ones who are best able to learn from failures.

How To Use Failures To Become Better

All of this brain signal stuff is good to know, but what's a product manager to do with this new knowledge? It turns out that it all relates to **what kind of person you are**.

Scientists believe that the world of product managers is **divided into two groups**: those of us with fixed mindsets and those of us with growth mindsets. A fixed mindset means that we think that we are as good as we're going to get at this product management thing. Those of us with growth mindsets believe that we can become better product managers.

Knowing about those brain signals, the scientists have done some studies. What they've found is that product managers with **a growth mindset** were generating a much larger Pe signal and were therefore able to learn more from the failures that they had.

I can almost hear what you are saying right now: great, **how can I get this "growth mindset"?** It turns out that it might be easier to do than you might think.

Product managers who surround themselves with people who are always telling them how smart they are seem to fall into the fixed mindset camp. However, those of us who surround ourselves with people who **complement us on our individual efforts** fall into the growth mindset camp. Being recognized for individual accomplishments seems to make a product manager want to understand why they've failed and to do better the next time around.

What All Of This Means For You

Every product manager will fail sometime. There's nothing that we can do about this: it could be a product launch that goes flat, a successful product that runs into a wall, or a competitor that shows up and takes our market away from us. The end result is the same: **we've failed**. You might not be willing to put this kind of experience on your product manager resume, but if you've been a product manager for any length of time it's happened to you.

What's important is how we handle this failure. Studies have shown that we have **two reactions to failure**: the immediate reaction and the one that follows it. Product managers who are going to be the most successful have a stronger response when they detect a failure and they then take the time to learn from their failure.

Taking the time to treat each failure as **a unique learning experience** is what allows some product managers to get ahead. If they've taken the time to surround themselves with people who praise them for their efforts, then they'll be able to turn every failure into a way to become better. Since we know that we're going to fail, this sure seems like a good thing to do! Now that's something that you can add to your product manager job description.

It's from the forge of failure that the steel of success is formed.

Hard Work Does Not Guarantee Success, But Success Does Not Happen Without Hard Work.

- Dr. Jim Anderson

Create Products Your Customers Want At A Price That They Are Willing To Pay!

Dr. Jim Anderson is available to provide training and coaching on the two topics that are the most important to product managers everywhere: how do I create the products that my customers want and what should I price them at?

Dr. Anderson believes that in order to both learn and remember what he says, product managers need to laugh. Each one of his speeches is full of fun and humor so that what he says "sticks" with everyone.

Dr. Anderson's Product Management Training Includes:

1. How can you segment your market?
2. What problems are your customers having right now?
3. Which of your customer's problems does your product solve?
4. How much of this problem does your product solve?
5. How much will it cost your customer if they don't fix this problem?

Dr. Jim Anderson presents over 100 speeches per year. To invite Dr. Anderson to speak at your event, contact him at:

Phone: 813-418-6970 or
Email: jim@BlueElephantConsulting.com

Photo Credits:

Cover - adrian valenzuela
https://www.flickr.com/photos/adrianv/

Chapter 1 - bearstache
https://www.flickr.com/photos/67285821@N02/

Chapter 2 - Tom Simpson
https://www.flickr.com/photos/randar/

Chapter 3 - takao goto
https://www.flickr.com/photos/48321994@N06/

Chapter 4 - Erica Cherup
https://www.flickr.com/photos/silvermarquis/

Chapter 5 - WFIU Public Radio
https://www.flickr.com/photos/wfiupublicradio/

Chapter 6 - Paul Mison
https://www.flickr.com/photos/blech/

Chapter 7 - Peter Miller
https://www.flickr.com/photos/pmillera4/

Chapter 8 - Elaine with Grey Cats
https://www.flickr.com/photos/elainegreycats/

Chapter 9 - Fabio
https://www.flickr.com/photos/star-dust/

Chapter 10 - Jen Crothers
https://www.flickr.com/photos/milopup/

Chapter 11 - Michael K
https://www.flickr.com/photos/vasto/

Chapter 12 - Sjoerd Wijn
https://www.flickr.com/photos/44974843@N04/

Other Books By The Author

Product Management

- How Product Managers Can Sell More Of Their Product: Tips & Techniques For Product Managers To Better Understand How To Sell Their Product

- How To Create A Successful Product That Customers Will Want: Techniques For Product Managers To Boost Product Sales And Increase Customer Satisfaction

- What Product Managers Need To Know About World-Class Product Development: How Product Managers Can Create Successful Products

- How Product Managers Can Learn To Understand Their Customers: Techniques For Product Managers To Better Understand What Their Customers Really Want

- Product Management Secrets: Techniques For Product Managers To Boost Produ Michael Kct Sales And Increase Customer Satisfaction

- Product Development Lessons For Product Managers: How Product Managers Can Create Successful Products

- Customer Lessons For Product Managers: Techniques For Product Managers To Better Understand What Their Customers Really Want

- Product Failure Lessons For Product Managers: Examples Of Products That Have Failed For Product Managers To Learn From

- Communication Skills For Product Managers: The Communication Skills That Product Managers Need To Know How To Use In Order To Have A Successful Product

- How To Have A Successful Product Manager Career: The Things That You Need To Be Doing TODAY In Order To Have A Successful Product Manager Career

- Product Manager Product Success: How to keep your product on track and make it become a success

Public Speaking

- Changing How You Speak To Overcome Your Fear Of Speaking: Change techniques that will transform a speech into a memorable event

- Delivering Excellence: How To Give Presentations That Make A Difference: Presentation techniques that will transform a speech into a memorable event

- Tools Speakers Need In Order To Give The Perfect Speech: What tools to use to create your next speech so that your message will be remembered forever!

- How To Create A Speech That Will Be Remembered

- Secrets To Organizing A Speech For Maximum Impact: How to put together a speech that will capture and hold your audience's attention

- How To Become A Better Speaker By Changing How You Speak: Change techniques that will transform a speech into a memorable event

- How To Give A Great Presentation: Presentation techniques that will transform a speech into a memorable event

- How To Rehearse In Order To Give The Perfect Speech: How to effectively rehearse your next speech to that your message be remembered forever!

- Secrets To Creating The Perfect Speech: How to create a speech that will make your message be remembered forever!

- Secrets To Organizing The Perfect Speech: How to organize the best speech of your life!

- Secrets To Planning The Perfect Speech: How to plan to give the best speech of your life

- How To Show What You Mean During A Presentation: How to use visual techniques to transform a speech into a memorable event

CIO Skills

- Keeping The Barbarians Out: How CIOs Can Secure Their Department and Company: Tips And Techniques For CIOs To Use In Order To Secure Both Their IT Department And Their Company

- What CIOs Need To Know In Order To Successfully Manage An IT Department: Decision Making Skills That Every CIO Needs To Have In Order To Be Able

To Make The Right Choices

- Becoming A Powerful And Effective Leader: Tips And Techniques That IT Managers Can Use In Order To Develop Leadership Skills

- CIO Secrets For Growing Innovation: Tips And Techniques For CIOs To Use In Order To Make Innovation Happen In Their IT Department

- Your Success As A CIO Depends On How Well You Communicate: Tips And Techniques For CIOs To Use In Order To Become Better Communicators

- What CIOs Need To Know About Working With Partners: Techniques For CIOs To Use In Order To Be Able To Successfully Work With Partners

- Critical CIO Management Skills: Decision Making Skills That Every CIO Needs To Have In Order To Be Able To Make The Right Choices

- How CIOs Can Make Innovation Happen: Tips And Techniques For CIOs To Use In Order To Make Innovation Happen In Their IT Department

- CIO Communication Skills Secrets: Tips And Techniques For CIOs To Use In Order To Become

Better Communicators

- Managing Your CIO Career: Steps That CIOs Have To Take In Order To Have A Long And Successful Career

- CIO Business Skills: How CIOs can work effectively with the rest of the company!

IT Manager Skills

- How To Build High Performance IT Teams: Tips And Techniques That IT Managers Can Use In Order To Develop Productive Teams

- Save Yourself, Save Your Job – How To Manage Your IT Career: Secrets That IT Managers Can Use In Order To Have A Successful Career

- Growing Your CIO Career: How CIOs Can Work With The Entire Company In Order To Be Successful

- How IT Managers Can Make Innovation Happen: Tips And Techniques For IT Managers To Use In Order To Make Innovation Happen In Their Teams

- Staffing Skills IT Managers Must Have: Tips And Techniques That IT Managers Can Use In Order To

Correctly Staff Their Teams

- Secrets Of Effective Leadership For IT Managers: Tips And Techniques That IT Managers Can Use In Order To Develop Leadership Skills

- IT Manager Career Secrets: Tips And Techniques That IT Managers Can Use In Order To Have A Successful Career

- IT Manager Budgeting Skills: How IT Managers Can Request, Manage, Use, And Track Their Funding

- Secrets Of Managing Budgets: What IT Managers Need To Know In Order To Understand How Their Company Uses Money

Negotiating

- Exploring How To Get The Deal That You Want In A Negotiation: How To Develop The Skill Of Exploring What Is Possible In A Negotiation In Order To Reach The Best Possible Deal

- Use The Power Of Arguing To Win Your Next Negotiation: How To Develop The Skill Of Effective Arguing In A Negotiation In Order To Get The Best Possible Outcome

- Learn How To Signal In Your Next Negotiation: How To Develop The Skill Of Effective Signaling In A Negotiation In Order To Get The Best Possible Outcome

- Learn The Skill Of Exploring In A Negotiation: How To Develop The Skill Of Exploring What Is Possible In A Negotiation In Order To Reach The Best Possible Deal

- Learn How To Argue In Your Next Negotiation: How To Develop The Skill Of Effective Arguing In A Negotiation In Order To Get The Best Possible Outcome|

- How To Open Your Next Negotiation: How To Start A Negotiation In Order To Get The Best Possible Outcome

- Preparing For Your Next Negotiation: What You Need To Do BEFORE A Negotiation Starts In Order To Get The Best Possible Deal

- Learn How To Package Trades In Your Next Negotiation

- All Good Things Come To An End: How To Close A Negotiation - How To Develop The Skill Of Closing In Order To Get The Best Possible Outcome From A

Negotiation

- Take No Prisoners In Your Next Negotiation: How To Start A Negotiation In Order To Get The Best Possible Outcome

Miscellaneous

- How To Heal A Broken Leg – Fast!: Understanding how to deal with a broken leg in order to start walking again quickly

- How Software Defined Networking (SDN) Is Going To Change Your World Forever: The Revolution In Network Design And How It Affects You

- The Power Of Virtualization: How It Affects Memory, Servers, and Storage: The Revolution In Creating Virtual Devices And How It Affects You

- The Internet-Enabled Successful School District Superintendent: How To Use The Internet To Boost Parental Involvement In Your Schools

- Power Distribution Unit (PDU) Secrets: What Everyone Who Works In A Data Center Needs To Know!

- Making The Jump: How To Land Your Dream Job When You Get Out Of College!

- How To Use The Internet To Create Successful Students And Involved Parents

"Practical, proven examples of how to secure the right product management job and be a success!"

> This book has been written with one goal in mind – to show you how to find the right product management job for you. We're going to show you how to make sure that this job turns into a success for you!
>
> **Let's Make Your Career A Success!**

What You'll Find Inside:

- **IS YOUR PRODUCT MANAGER RESUME IPHONE READY?**

- **3 SKILLS THAT MOST PRODUCT MANAGERS ARE MISSING**

- **BREAKTHROUGH IN SOLVING THE PROBLEM OF HOW TO EVALUATE A PRODUCT MANAGER**

- **PRODUCT MANAGERS NEED TO LEARN HOW TO FAIL**

Dr. Jim Anderson brings his 4 college degrees coupled with over 25 years of real-world experience to this book. He's managed products at some of the world's largest firms as well as at start-ups. He's going to show you what you need to do in order to make your career a success!

www.ingramcontent.com/pod-product-compliance
Lightning Source LLC
Chambersburg PA
CBHW061200180526
45170CB00002B/882